I dedicate this book to the late, but greatest creative cook, Ruth Scott Mackey; my mom I love and miss her so much!

A BAND OF GOLD FREE-DA

INGREDIENTS
Orange Bell Pepper, White Onions, Chicken Chunks, Jasmine Rice, Fresh String Beans, Garlic and The Legendary Cheryl Scott's Seasoning

HOW IT'S MADE
Boil water with Olive Oil and a dash of Legendary Cheryl Scott's Seasoning. When water boils add some jasmine rice in just below the water. Let water boil on medium to high, when water evaporates turn stove on low and cover pot and let rice steam until cooked. Cut up chicken into chunks and season with the Legendary Cheryl Scott's seasoning. Slice some white onions and orange bell pepper. In a wok or large frying pan add some olive oil to heat and stir fry chicken chunks, onions, and bell pepper for 5 to 7 min on medium heat. Then heat wok with olive oil and add fresh cut string beans to stir fry with garlic and butter and of course the Legendary Cheryl Scott's seasoning. Cook string beans until soft and Enjoy!

NO *Measuring* COOKBOOK

by the Legendary Cheryl Scott

© 2022 Legendary Cheryl Scott. All rights reserved.

No part of this book may be reproduced, stored in a retrieval system, or transmitted by any means without the written permission of the author.

AuthorHouse™
1663 Liberty Drive
Bloomington, IN 47403
www.authorhouse.com
Phone: 833-262-8899

Because of the dynamic nature of the Internet, any web addresses or links contained in this book may have changed since publication and may no longer be valid. The views expressed in this work are solely those of the author and do not necessarily reflect the views of the publisher, and the publisher hereby disclaims any responsibility for them.

Any people depicted in stock imagery provided by Getty Images are models, and such images are being used for illustrative purposes only.
Certain stock imagery © Getty Images.

This book is printed on acid-free paper.

ISBN: 978-1-6655-7500-3 (sc)
ISBN: 978-1-6655-7501-0 (hc)
ISBN: 978-1-6655-7499-0 (e)

Library of Congress Control Number: 2022920640

Print information available on the last page.

Published by AuthorHouse 11/03/2022

authorHOUSE

MACKEY BOY'S BOIL FISH

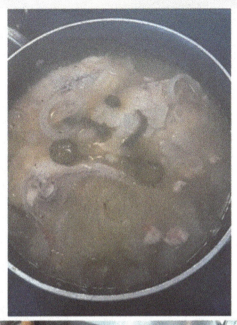

INGREDIENTS
Fresh Cut Grouper Fish Steaks, White onions Jalapeño pepper, Lemon Juice, Bacon, Legendary Cheryl Scott's seasoning

HOW IT'S MADE
Season Grouper Fish Steaks first with the Legendary Cheryl Scott's seasoning and let sit for about 30 min for seasoning to take. Put some water to boil. Fry bacon in a large skillet, when bacon is cooked pour hot boiling water in skillet, add in seasoned grouper fish steaks. Then add sliced onions jalapeno peppers and lemon juice. Let boil on medium for 8 to 10 minutes and there you have it

LONDON'S LOBSTER SEAFOOD PLATTER

INGREDIENTS
Lobster tails, French Fries, Shrimp, The Legendary Cheryl Scott's seasoning (spicy or mild), Self-rising white flour, Vegetable oil

HOW IT'S MADE
First, season lobster tails with The Legendary Cheryl Scott's spicy or mild seasoning then, season the shrimps separately. Place the seasoned lobster tails and shrimps in a bag of self-rising white flour. Heat deep fryer to approximately 450°, drop the lobster tails and shrimps in the hot vegetable oil for about five minutes, after all lobster tails and shrimps are cooked remove and put in french fries. Let french fries cook for about 4 to 5 minutes, remove and strain oil and there you have it.

ANGELA'S DELICIOUS STUFFING

INGREDIENTS
Large Green and Yellow Bell peppers in fact any color peppers you like. White onions, additional Green, Yellow, Red bell peppers, Ground beef, Kosher salt and of course Legendary Cheryl Scott's Seasonings

HOW IT'S MADE
Cut in half large bell peppers. Then on the side dice up bell peppers and onions. Put in medium heated wok ground beef, diced bell peppers, onions and seasonings. Cook until done. Stuff cooked ground beef in large cut bell pepper halves. Put a little water in baking pan and then place stuffed peppers on baking pan and let bake for 17 to 20 minutes. A quick delicious meal for the family!

ASHLEY'S CREAMY GRITS

INGREDIENTS
Grits, Butter, Chicken broth, Heavy whip cream

HOW IT'S MADE
Boil chicken broth for 7 to 8 minutes, then throw in some heavy whip cream, then throw in the grits and some butter and let it cook for 15 to 17 minutes slowly. And Wala there you have it creamy grits. I like cooking my grits a little longer because, me The Legendary Cheryl Scott loves creamy soft grits. I dedicate these creamy grits to one of my favorite niece Ashley Jordan. And there you have it!

ASK BERNIE BEE

INGREDIENTS
Shrimps, Green peppers, Yellow peppers, Red peppers, Special olive oil and the Legendary Cheryl Scott's seasoning

HOW IT'S MADE
Put some olive oil in a pan, stir fry yellow, green, and red bell peppers for about 2 -1/2 minutes, then throw in the shrimps and let sauté about another two minutes and bam there you have asked Bernie

ATLANTIS SALMON

INGREDIENTS
Salmon steaks, Onions, Fresh parsley, Lemon juice, Garlic butter, Parmesan cheese and of course the Legendary Cheryl Scott's seasoning

HOW IT'S MADE
Take as many pieces of salmon steaks as you want. In this dish I used five pieces of salmon steaks. Season salmon with the Legendary Cheryl Scott's seasoning. Place in the oven at 350 degrees and let it bake for seven minutes or until golden brown. This is named after my niece Atlantis because when she spends the night over, she loves herself some salmon.

BABY CHRIS PARMESAN CHICKEN WINGS

INGREDIENTS
Chicken Flats, Chicken drumettes, Garlic butter, Parmesan cheese, Legendary Cheryl Scott's seasoning

HOW IT'S MADE
Season chicken drumettes and flats with Legendary Cheryl Scott's Seasoning. Deep fry chicken flats and drumettes until golden brown. Add garlic butter and the Parmesan cheese over the wings and place them on a plate. I named this dish after my only grandson Charlie Chris because he loves himself some wings

NACHELLELOVETHEDOLPHINS BAKED STEWED YELLOWTAILS

INGREDIENTS

Filet yellow tail, Shrimps, White onions, Yellow, Orange and Red bell peppers, Stewed tomatoes, Tomato sauce, Olive oil, Legendary Cheryl Scott's seasoning spicy or mild, fresh parsley, cayenne pepper

HOW IT'S MADE

First, heat some olive oil in a medium frying pan then place yellow tail in pan and sprinkle The Legendary Cheryl Scott's seasoning over the yellow tail and let brown a little on each side. Leave yellowtail in pan and take the red, orange, and yellow bell peppers cut them up and put them over the yellow tail, then add the onions, add some stew tomatoes, some tomato sauce and a half a cup of water and let simmer for about 7 to 8 minutes. Add shrimp, some cayenne pepper, and some cut up fresh parsley. Transfer everything to a long aluminum pan, turn oven on to 350° and, let it cook for 15 to 18 minutes. You will never taste yellowtails so scrumptious!

RENICE'S BROCCOLI AND CHEESE BAKED POTATO

INGREDIENTS
Baked potato, Broccoli, Cheddar cheese and Legendary Cheryl Scott's Seasonings

HOW IT'S MADE
On top of the stove let potatoes boil for about 10 minutes. Move the potato out of the pot and wrap the potato up in aluminum foil, put it in oven on 350° and let bake for 30 minutes. If potatoes are a little big let bake for approximately 15 more minutes, then remove the baked potato out of the oven. Slice potato in the middle and in another pan stir-fry some broccoli with butter and put it on top of the potato. Add in Legendary Cheryl Scott's seasoning, add some cheddar cheese on top put it back in the oven for approximately three minutes and there you have. Bernie loves bake potato and broccoli

BEVERLY'S MILKY FRIED CONCH

INGREDIENTS
Conch, Milk, Flour, Lawry salt.

HOW IT'S MADE
Be sure to have conch tenderize 4 times at the fish market. Soak tenderized conch in milk, remove the conch from the milk and add the Lawry salt to the flour. Be sure to have your oil on and heated. Dip the conch in the seasoned flour, shake off all the excess flour and place it in a basket in the deep fryer. Fry until it is golden brown. It should take approximately 4 to 5 minutes. Remove it from the basket, place it on a plate and there you have it Beverly's milky fried conch. This is one of her favorite fried conch

CHARLIE CHRIS III CRAB BOIL

INGREDIENTS
Snow crab legs, Garlic, Fresh parsley, Parmesan cheese, Butter, Legendary Cheryl Scott's seasoning

HOW IT'S MADE
Boil some water and add in crab legs for about seven minutes then take them out of the pot. In a medium pan sauté some fresh garlic, fresh parsley, butter, and Legendary Cheryl Scott's seasoning. On medium heat throw in the crab legs and mixed it all together when done lay the crab legs in a long pan. Add in the Parmesan cheese on top and there you have it Charlie's crab boil. Sometimes he like to eat the crabs all to himself because, he's the only grandson and he is spoiled.

CHERGREGORY'S LUNCH SPECIALS

INGREDIENTS

Lettuce, Spinach, Salmon and Shrimps, Legendary Cheryl Scott's seasoning, Olive oil

HOW IT'S MADE

Season some shrimps and salmon with Legendary Cheryl Scott's seasoning. Heat in a large frying pan some olive oil and grill shrimps and salmon. Remove from the stove and let cool. While waiting for the salmon and shrimp to cool, cut up some lettuce and spinach add to a takeout bowl place the shrimps and salmon on top of the lettuce and spinach then sprinkle a little of my special Legendary Cheryl Scott seasoning on top and wow this is the results. And this is another one of Dr. CG Hines lunch.

CHERGREGORY'S HEALTHY OMELETTE

INGREDIENTS:
Chicken chunks, Olive oil, Egg whites, Spinach, Cheddar cheese, Legendary Cheryl Scott's seasoning

HOW IT'S MADE
First, fry chicken chunks in some olive oil, put that aside then, take some egg whites and put it in the frying pan next, put the cheddar cheese, then take the chicken chunks and place it on the eggs and cheddar cheese. Last but not least add spinach and my mild Legendary Cheryl Scott's seasoning. This is a healthy choice omelet because My baby girl Chergregory love to eat Healthy.

CHERYL DENISE

INGREDIENTS
Mashed potatoes, Salmon, Onions, Parsley, Shrimps, Heavy whip cream, Garlic and Butter, Olive oil, The Legendary Cheryl Scott's Seasoning

HOW IT'S MADE
First, season the salmon and shrimps with the Legendary Cheryl Scott's seasoning. Heat olive oil in medium frying pan and sauté salmon, shrimps, and onions altogether. Throw in some parsley and my spicy Legendary Cheryl Scott's seasoning. Place over a bed of mashed potatoes with some heavy whip cream and some garlic butter to make a gravy and believe me it is awesome! I name this dish after me Cheryl Denise. Because I love myself some salmon and homemade mashed potatoes with onions and all those delicious toppings.

RODDY-DEE'S GOLDEN FRIED CHICKEN WINGS

INGREDIENTS
Chicken wings, Legendary Cheryl Scott's seasoning mild or spicy Seasoning, Flour, Garlic, and Salt

HOW IT'S MADE
You can either use a deep fryer or a frying pan it's your choice. Season your chicken with the Legendary Cheryl Scott's seasoning, garlic, and salt. Add some vegetable oil in deep fryer then put seasoned chicken wings in flour and place them in deep fryer. Fry chicken until golden brown and there you have it...

CHERYL DENISE SCOTT MEAN GREENS SPICY

INGREDIENTS
Fresh cut greens, Smoked turkey necks, Onions, Jalapeño peppers, Crystal hot sauce, Legendary Cheryl Scott's seasoning, Kosher salt

HOW IT'S MADE
Wash and cut up collard greens, then placed them in boiling water. Also throw in some smoked turkey necks, Legendary Cheryl Scott's seasoning, some jalapeño peppers and just a pinch of kosher salt and onions. I also added 10 drops of Crystal hot sauce. And there you have it my CDS mean greens.

MISSING MY DEATRICK CHICKEN CRAB FRIED RICE

INGREDIENTS
Chicken, shrimp, Red peppers, Green peppers, Legendary Cheryl Scott's seasoning spicy or mild, Vegetable oil, Uncle Ben rice, Tomato sauce or Tomato paste, Kitchen bouquet

HOW IT'S MADE
First, boil some water then and add some kitchen bouquet while water is boiling then, add the Uncle Bens rice. While rice is cooking sauté some red and green bell peppers. Cut up some chicken breast into cubes. On the side in a medium pan heat some vegetable oil and stir fry chicken chunks and shrimps. Set that aside until the rice is done. When rice is finished pour it in a long Aluminum pan then add the sauté green and red peppers, chicken chunks and shrimps. Last add my Legendary Cheryl Scott's mild or spicy seasoning. Mix it all together wow and there you have it.

CHILD THAT'S THEM NASSAU CONCH FRITTERS

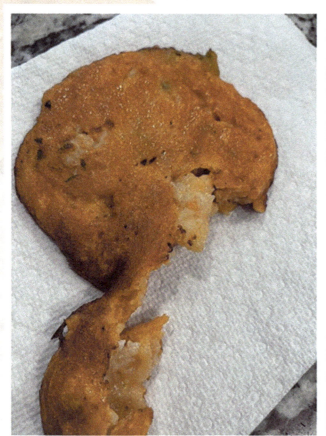

INGREDIENTS
Bahamian conch, Red bell peppers, Green bell peppers, Onions, Eggs, Ketchup, Crystal hot sauce, Lawry's salt, Cayenne pepper

HOW IT'S MADE
Dice up all the Bahamian conch and put it in one mixing bowl. Add in the mixing bowl water, eggs, lots of cayenne pepper, self-rising flour, diced red and green bell peppers, diced onions, salt, a dash of black pepper, Crystal hot sauce and ketchup. Heat some vegetable oil in a frying pan and drop some of the mixture in pan. Fry to my perfection golden brown and sprinkle some parsley flakes over the conch fritters and there you have it Walla!

COME ON ASIA

INGREDIENTS
Lobster tails, Steak, Penne noodles, Butter, Garlic, Green onions, Heavy whip cream, Legendary Cheryl Scott's seasoning

HOW IT'S MADE
First, boil the noodles and set them aside. Boil some lobster tails until fully cooked. Cube up some steak and season with the Legendary Cheryl Scott's seasoning. Also cut up some green onions. Next in a medium frying pan stir fry green onions and seasoned steak strips. Cook for about 3 to 4 minutes then add some heavy whip cream. Take the noodles and add to the stir fry of green onions and steak strips and let this mixture continue to cook for an additional 6 to 8 minutes. Take the boil lobsters and put them on top of that pasta and there you have it.

COREY'S CONCH CRAB BALLS

INGREDIENTS

Conch, Real crab meat, Onions, Red bell peppers, Self-rising flour, Townhouse crackers, Eggs, Breadcrumbs, Legendary Cheryl Scott's mile seasoning, Vegetable oil

HOW IT'S MADE

First, place cut up small conch chunks in a mixing bowl. Then add to mixing bowl real crab meat, townhouse crackers, eggs, breadcrumbs, self-rising flour and of course the Legendary Cheryl Scott's mild seasoning. Put some vegetable oil in a pan on medium heat, scooped the mixture out with a small ice cream scooper, fry until golden brown and there you have it. A wonderful treat!

DEE MONEY $$ SPICY SAUSAGE PASTA

INGREDIENTS
Penne noodles, Georgia sausage, Spinach, Legendary Cheryl Scott's seasoning, Shrimps, Cayenne pepper, Garlic butter, Minced garlic, Heavy whip cream

HOW IT'S MADE
Boil the noodles first. Slice up and fry some Georgia sausage, after they are fully cooked then add some garlic butter, minced garlic, some baby spinach, and shrimp. Stir in some heavy whip cream and let simmer on the stove. Drain the noodles then put it in a long aluminum pan, stir in the Georgia sausage and shrimp stir fry and all the nice spicy seasonings especially the Legendary Cheryl Scott's seasoning. I name this after the love of my life of 25 years THE DUDE

DINNER FOR THE QUEEN

INGREDIENTS
Idaho potato, Shrimps, Broccoli, The Legendary Cheryl Scott's seasoning spicy or mild, Cheddar cheese, Garlic butter

HOW IT'S MADE
First take an Idaho potato put some holes in it with a fork then, put it on a cookie sheet in the oven on 375°. Let it bake for approximately 25 to 27 minutes. While that is baking, stir-fry some large shrimps with some garlic butter sauce then, add in the broccoli. When bake potato is done cut it open, add in some garlic butter, the shrimps, broccoli, and some cheddar cheese on top. Put potato with filling back in the oven and let it bake for another five minutes and you will have a big potato fit for a queen that's me The Legendary Cheryl Scott.

DION NICHOLAS CHICKEN TENDERS

INGREDIENTS
Chicken breast strips, Garlic butter, Italian seasoning, The Legendary Cheryl Scott's seasoning mild or spicy, Orange bell peppers, Butter

HOW IT'S MADE
In a large frying pan sauté chicken strip, then add some garlic butter and butter, toss in orange bell peppers, and add in Italian seasoning and of course the Legendary Cheryl Scott's seasoning mild or spicy. Let it cook for about 7 to 8 minutes and there you have it you can either eat it over a bed of white rice or mashed potatoes. This one was named after my nephew Dion Nicolas because when he was growing up that's all he wanted to eat was chicken tenders and there you have it.

DR. CHERGREGORY'S FAVORITE

INGREDIENTS
Shrimps, Onions, Red bell pepper, Olive oil, Chicken broth, The Legendary Cheryl Scott's seasoning spicy or mild, Uncle Ben rice, Soy sauce

HOW IT'S MADE
First in a small pot boil some Uncle Ben's white rice in some chicken broth and water. Let boil for approximately 7 to 8 minutes then let it simmer for another 8 to 9 minutes. In a medium frying pan heat some olive oil and stir fry some onions, red bell peppers, medium shrimps, and sauté for approximately 3 to 5 minutes. After rice is done pour stir fry of sautéed shrimp, bell pepper, onions mix altogether and add in The Legendary Cheryl Scott spicy seasoning or mild. Also add in a couple of drops of soy sauce stir it all together and there you have it! If you have some extra shrimps bell pepper and onions, put it on top of the rice and Wala It is delicious! And that's another one of Legendary Cheryl Scott favorite dish.

GARLIC SHRIMP AND CRAB BOIL

INGREDIENTS
Snow crab legs, Medium shrimps, Garlic butter, Fresh garlic, Butter, garlic butter, The Legendary Cheryl Scott's seasoning spicy or mild

HOW IT'S MADE
First preheat oven to 375°, then in a large Aluminum pan add snow crabs and shrimp, The Legendary Cheryl Scott's seasoning spicy or mild, garlic butter, regular butter, and fresh garlic. Put it in the oven and let it bake approximately 9 to 10 minutes and there you have it. Awesome dish for family and friends gathering

GARY'S BUTTER SHRIMP AND GRITS

INGREDIENTS
Large shrimps, White onions, Garlic butter, Fresh squeezed lemon, Parsley flakes, Pepper seeds, The Legendary Cheryl Scott's spicy or mild seasoning, Grits

HOW IT'S MADE
First, in a medium pot boil some water for approximately 5 to 7 minutes then add grits. Stir it so you will not have any lumps, add some butter, add some whipping cream, and let it simmer for approximately 20 to 22 minutes. Next in a medium frying pan sauté some shrimp in garlic butter, add some cut up onions, some parsley flakes, squeeze some fresh lemon over it and some pepper seeds and of course The Legendary Cheryl Scott spicy or mild seasoning. Let it simmer for approximately 3 to 4 minutes. When the shrimp dish is done put it on bed of grits and there you have it, that's one of my favorites or a Saturday morning!

GOOD MORNING SUNSHINE

INGREDIENTS
Salmon fillet, Red and Green bell peppers, Onions, Idaho potatoes, Grits, Chicken broth, Kosher salt, Heavy whip cream, Self-rising flour and The Legendary Cheryl Scott seasoning spicy or mild, Vegetable oil

HOW IT'S MADE
First in a medium pot take some chicken broth along with some heavy whip cream and some butter and let boil for approximately 3 to 4 minutes then add a dash of kosher salt and grits. Please do not forget The Legendary Cheryl Scott's seasoning, just a dash of the mild or spicy. While that is cooking, next take two Idaho potatoes and boil until they are soft. Put potatoes in a bowl and take a spoon to mashed them up into small chunky pieces, add in diced red and green bell peppers. Heat vegetable oil in a small frying pan and add in salmon fillet. Toss it on its side for approximately one minute each side. Remove from pan and shred the salmon and add it to the mashed potatoes. Don't forget the Legendary Cheryl Scott's seasoning spicy or mild. Take a dash of self-rising flour and create a firm pasty batter. Take and make patties from batter. Heat vegetable oil in deep fryer and fry patties for approximately 3 to 4 minutes. When done put it over a bed of the best creamy, buttery grits you have ever tasted and there you have it that's another one of The Legendary Cheryl Scott's favorites.

GREGORY'S GOLDEN FRIED PORK CHOP

INGREDIENTS
Center cut pork chops, Legendary Cheryl Scott's seasoning, Black pepper, Self-rising flour, Vegetable oil

HOW IT'S MADE
Season pork chops with The Legendary Cheryl Scott's seasoning mild or spicy your choice and add black pepper. Take each individual chop and add flour on both sides, shake off excess flour. Heat skillet with some vegetable oil. Fry chops for 3 to 5 minutes on each side until golden brown. This is a nice entrée with rice and veggies of your choice. And there you have it.

HIS AND HERS SALMON OVER A BED OF PASTA

INGREDIENTS
Salmon, Baby spinach, Chicken broth, Garlic, Egg noodles, The Legendary Cheryl Scott's seasoning spicy or mild, Olive oil, Garlic butter

HOW IT'S MADE
Boil egg noodles in some chicken broth and water. While that is boiling in a small saucepan sauté some salmon and shrimps with The Legendary Cheryl Scott's seasoning, put some garlic, some baby spinach, and garlic butter. Dice up fresh parsley after the noodles are finished. Put noodles in a bowl take spinach, garlic, shrimp, salmon dish and pour it over the egg noodles. Top it off with some diced parsley and there you have a dish for him and for her.

HEALTHY CHOICES

INGREDIENTS
Baby spinach, Cucumbers, Mozzarella cheese, Shrimp, Chicken strips, Chopped up chicken, Broccoli, Garlic, and the Legendary Cheryl Scott's seasoning mild or spicy, Olive oil

HOW IT'S MADE
Put some fresh spinach in a dish, cut up some cucumbers on the side. Sauté a split open chicken breast, some chicken chunks, some shrimps and broccoli with the Legendary Cheryl Scott's seasonings mild or spicy. Add broccoli, mozzarella cheese and or cheddar cheese. It's a healthy choice when you can create several different dishes of your choice. On a bed of fresh baby spinach with cucumbers on the side and sprinkled with a little mozzarella cheese, you can have the chicken breast with shrimp or without. You can have it on a bed of baby spinach with seasoned chicken chunks or chicken strips. And there you have it 1, 2, 3, 4 healthy choices.

HOT MAMA SPICY SALMON AND SHRIMP

INGREDIENTS
Salmon steaks, Large shrimps, The Legendary Cheryl Scott's spicy seasoning, Olive oil, Cayenne pepper

HOW IT'S MADE
Season salmon steaks and shrimps with the Legendary Cheryl Scott's spicy seasoning along with cayenne pepper. Place salmon steak in the skillet on some medium heat with olive oil. Turn on each side back and forth for possibly 2 to 4 minutes or eight to my perfection. Then remove salmon steaks and add in seasoned shrimps. Sauté until done. I usually eat this over a bit of yellow rice or lettuce and spinach with some mozzarella cheese. And there you have it. Real simple right!

I AM THE LEGEND CHERYL SCOTT

INGREDIENTS
Salmon, Shrimp, Lettuce, Spinach, Yellow rice, Chicken broth, The Legendary Cheryl Scott's seasoning spicy or mild, Italian seasoning, Thyme

HOW IT'S MADE
In a small pot take some Uncle Ben's yellow rice and let boil in a pot of water, chicken broth and some butter for approximately 15 to 17, then let simmer on medium low until cooked. While that is cooking in a skillet sauté salmon fillet and some shrimps. Season with Italian seasoning and the Legendary Cheryl Scott's seasoning mild. While that is cooking on a medium low heat, take some lettuce and baby spinach place it on a plate then add salmon and shrimp on top. Add a scoop of Uncle Ben's yellow rice on the side. Sprinkle some Legendary Cheryl Scott seasonings on top of everything and there you have it because I am the Legend.

I GET IT FROM MY MAMA CRAB BOIL

INGREDIENTS
Crab claws, Shrimps, Corn on the cob, Georgia sausage mild or spicy, Baby white potatoes, Fresh parsley, The Legendary Cheryl Scott's seasoning spicy or mild, Fresh garlic, Garlic butter

HOW IT'S MADE
First boil corn on the cob with some butter. In a frying pan fry some Georgia sausage mild or spicy. In a large aluminum pan toss in the Georgia sausage, crab claws, corn on the cob, baby white potatoes, shrimp, fresh parsley, fresh garlic, The Legendary Cheryl Scott's spicy or mild seasoning, and garlic butter. Mix it all together in large aluminum pan preheat oven to 300°. Cover aluminum pan, let bake for approximately 15 to 20 minutes and there you have it. This is a serious meal. Don't hurt yourself!

I'M HAVING A MOMENT

INGREDIENTS
Salmon fillet, Tricolor bell peppers, Green onions, Garlic butter, Legendary Cheryl Scott's seasoning spicy or mild, Creamy whip cream

HOW IT'S MADE
In a large skillet sauté garlic butter, tricolor bell peppers with, The Legendary Cheryl Scott's spicy seasoning. Add in the salmon fillet with some green onions, and a little creamy whip cream. Let simmer for about 10 to 13 minutes and there you have it. You can either eat this over some rice or some egg Noodles which ever you prefer.

I'M JUST LAQUASHIA

INGREDIENTS
Shrimps or Chicken, Large noodles, Chicken broth, Fresh parsley, Garlic butter, Fresh garlic, The Legendary Cheryl Scott's mild seasoning, Heavy whip cream

HOW IT'S MADE
Boil noodles in some chicken broth. In a large frying take some garlic butter, fresh garlic, fresh parsley flakes, The Legendary Cheryl Scott's seasoning mild put in some heavy whip cream, let it cook for approximately 2 to 4 minutes. Add in shrimps, chicken or both whichever you prefer and let it cook for about a minute or so, then add in noodles mix it all together and there you have it

IT RUNS IN THE MACKEY FAMILY

INGREDIENTS
Medium shrimps, Imitation crab, Italian sausage, The Legendary Cheryl Scott's seasoning mild or spicy, Red peppers seeds, Garlic butter, Olive Oil

HOW IT'S MADE
First sauté some Italian sausages in a frying pan with olive oil. Add imitation crab, then shrimps and season with The Legendary Cheryl Scott's seasoning, along with the garlic butter and some red peppers seeds. With this recipe you have a choice, you can eat only Italian sausage or garlic shrimp or garlic imitation crab or you can have all three of them it's your choice. It was in my family however; I usually eat all three of them on a bed of rice.

IT TAKES TWO JOHNNY

INGREDIENTS
Salmon steak, Large jumbo shrimps, Cayenne pepper, The Legendary Cheryl Scott's spicy seasoning Lemon, Fresh garlic, Olive oil

HOW IT'S MADE
Season salmon and shrimps with The Legendary Cheryl Scott's seasoning spicy, also use some cayenne pepper. Heat olive oil in a large frying pan. Add in salmon and let cook for 3 minutes on both sides, then add the shrimps for about 2 to 3 minutes. Put all in aluminum pan squeeze some lemon over it and put it in the oven on 375° and let it bake for 8 to 9 minutes and there you have it.

JERK JOSEPHINE PIGEON PEAS AND RICE

INGREDIENTS
Uncle Ben converted white rice, Green bell pepper, Pigeon peas, Kitchen bouquet, chicken broth, Jerk seasoning, The Legendary Cheryl Scott's seasoning, spicy or mild, Thyme Cayenne pepper, Vegetable oil

HOW IT WAS MADE
First in a large pot fry some bell pepper is some vegetable oil then add some pigeon peas, kitchen bouquet, jerk seasoning, and The Legendary Cheryl Scott's seasoning spicy or mild. Also, add some chicken broth and water and bring it to a boil on medium for about 3 to 4 minutes. Then add the uncle Ben Rice and bring to a boil for about 3 to 4 minutes. Stirred the pot then put a lid over the pot let it cook on low medium for approximately 15 to 18 minutes and there you have it.

KAY'S FAVORITE

INGREDIENTS
Orange, Red and Orange bell peppers, Onions, Italian sausage, Shrimps, Tomato sauce, The Legendary Cheryl Scott's spicy seasoning, Cayenne pepper, Imitation crab, Vegetable oil

HOW IT WAS MADE
In a large skillet heat some vegetable oil and fry Italian sausage, onions, red and orange bell peppers. Add in The Legendary Cheryl Scott's spicy seasoning, two cans of tomato sauce then add the imitation crab and shrimp. Let it simmer for about 3 to 4 minutes and there you have it you can eat this over a bed of rice or some mashed potatoes. You can even put it over a baked potato and there you have it KAYS favorite

KEITH DON'T FORGET TO EAT YOUR VEGETABLES

INGREDIENTS
French cut string beans, Garlic butter, Fresh pork bacon, Chicken broth, The Legendary Cheryl Scott's seasoning spicy or mild, Vegetable oil

HOW IT WAS MADE
First, in a medium pan heat some vegetable oil, add in some fresh cut bacon. After bacon sauté for 2 to 3 minutes add in French cut green beans and mix in some Legendary Cheryl Scott's spicy seasoning spicy or mild. Add some garlic butter, some chicken broth and let simmer for approximately 30 to 45 minutes on medium and there you have it whenever my nephew came over for dinner this was one of his specialties(LOL) because he didn't like to eat his vegetables.

KEVIN'S AUNTIE I'M HUNGRY

INGREDIENTS
Shrimp, Spaghetti noodles, Onions, Red, Orange, Green bell peppers, Soy sauce, Vegetable broth, The Legendary Cheryl Scott spicy or mild, Vegetable oil

HOW IT WAS MADE
First boil some spaghetti noodles and some vegetable broth together. While that is cooking in a small frying pan, sauté some shrimps, orange, red, green bell peppers with The Legendary Cheryl Scott's seasoning spicy or mild. Also add some garlic butter. Let that simmer on a low stove, then drain the spaghetti noodles and add it to the small frying pan. Stir-fry it all up with some soy sauce and there you have it Kevin's auntie I'm hungry!

LADY WHAT'S FOR DINNER

INGREDIENTS
Salmon steak, Spinach, Onions, Bell peppers, Yellow grits, Parsley flakes, The Legendary Cheryl Scott's season spicy or mild, Heavy whipping cream, Chicken broth, red peppers

HOW IT'S MADE
First boil some grits in a medium pot with some chicken broth and Heavy whipping cream. Then I added some yellow flavor seasoning for the grits, some garlic butter, some kosher salt, and let it cook for approximately 25 to 35 minutes on A medium stove. While that is cooking season salmon with the Legendary Cheryl Scott's seasoning spicy or mild. In a medium frying pan add bell peppers, onions, and parsley flakes. After the grits is done put on a plate add some fresh spinach on top then put the salmon and all the spices and herbs on top of the fresh baby spinach, I sprinkle some more parsley flakes and there you have it. My oldest daughter always call me and say Lady what's for dinner.

LISA'S FAVORITE SEAFOOD RICE

INGREDIENTS
Uncle Ben-white rice, Red bell peppers, Green bell peppers, Medium shrimp, Imitation crab, Chicken broth, The Legendary Cheryl Scott's seasoning spicy or mild, Yellow seasoning

HOW IT'S MADE
First bring some water and chicken broth to a boil for approximately 5 to 8 minutes. Then add the yellow seasoning and let it warm up for another 2 to 3 minutes then add Uncle Ben's white rice. Let it boil and cook on medium low for approximately 25 minutes. In a large frying pan stir fry some green and red bell peppers, imitation crab meat, add the shrimps and stir-fry it. Use the Legendary Cheryl Scott's seasoning spicy or mild. While the rice is cooling down let the shrimp and all the good seasoning cook for approximately 2 to 3 more minutes then set that aside and take the rice out of the pot and put it in a medium size aluminum pan. Pour all the toppings all over the yellow rice add some more Legendary Cheryl Scott's seasoning spicy or mild mix it all together and there you have it. This is one of my favorites I love to make this.

LET'S GET IT ON MARVIN J.

INGREDIENTS
Chicken Chunks, Georgia sausages mild or hot, The Legendary Cheryl Scott's seasoning spicy or mild, Tomato sauce, Bell peppers, Vegetable oil, Onions

HOW IT'S MADE
Cut up chicken breast into chunks and season with the Legendary Cheryl Scott's seasoning. Also, sauté Georgia sausages in another pan. Cut up onions and bell peppers. Heat medium skillet with vegetable oil, throw in seasoned chicken chunks, onions, bell peppers and Georgia sausages. Let it cook for approximately 8 to 10 minutes on low heat then there you have it. You can either eat this over a bed of rice of your choice.

NEASE'S DICEY SPICY MASHED POTATOES

INGREDIENTS
Idaho potatoes, Whipping cream, Fresh parsley, Garlic butter, Legendary Cheryl Scott's spicy seasoning, water

HOW IT'S MADE
Cut up five Idaho potatoes, boil them with skin on in water until soft. Peel potatoes and set them aside. In a bowl put some water not too much, add in the heavy whipped cream and the peeled potatoes and mashed them up together. Add in the spicy Legendary Cheryl Scott's seasoning along with some garlic butter, fresh parsley and there you have it

NETTIE BOO WORLD'S FAMOUS LASAGNA

INGREDIENTS
Lasagna Pasta, Ground beef, Spaghetti sauce, Ricotta cheese, Two eggs, Mozzarella cheese, Cheddar cheese, Fresh parsley

HOW IT'S MADE
First, heat large skillet and begin to brown ground beef. While that's cooking mix together ricotta cheese and two eggs in a bowl with a sprinkle of mozzarella cheese. After ground beef finish browning drain off the fat and season to your taste. Add spaghetti sauce and let simmer for 10 minutes. Next scoop out one cup of sauce and pour in the bottom of the pan, then put a layer of uncooked lasagna pasta, spread ricotta cheese mixture on top of noodles then pour about 2 cups of meat sauce on top, then add cheese mixture repeat this step two more times after your third layer cover top and place in oven on 350 degrees and let cook for 55 minutes. When done, add the balance of mozzarella cheese, cheddar cheese and parsley on top. Put back in oven so cheese can melt. When you start to see cheese, bubble remove from oven and let rest for 15 to 20 minutes and there you have it my lasagna.

RUDY'S SPICY CHUNKY SALMON SATURDAY NIGHT SPECIAL

INGREDIENTS
Salmon, Chicken chunks, Fresh parsley, The Legendary Cheryl Scott's spicy or mild seasoning, Instant mashed potatoes, Chicken broth, Garlic butter, Baby spinach, Olive oil, Heavy whipping cream

HOW IT'S MADE
Boil some chicken broth and heavy whip cream together. Add some of the Legendary Cheryl Scott's seasoning spicy or mild, some garlic butter and let boil for approximately 5 to 7 minutes then add instant mashed potatoes and stir to my perfection. While that is cooking on low heat, in a medium frying pan put some olive oil and season salmon, chicken chunks to my perfection. Put them in the olive oil for approximately 4 to 5 minutes then add heavy whipping cream with The Legendary Cheryl Scott's spicy seasoning let it all simmer for about 2 minutes then set it aside. After the mashed potatoes are cooked put it on a plate then add all the good toppings on top of the mashed potatoes and there you have it.

RUTH ANN'S BOHEMIAN PARSLEY POTATOES

INGREDIENTS
Red potatoes, Fresh parsley, Minced garlic, Legendary Cheryl Scott's seasoning spicy or mild, Garlic butter. Salt, Pepper

HOW IT'S MADE
First cut up about 6 to 7 red potatoes in chunks. Put them to boil in some water approximately 10 to 17 minutes then remove from stove and drain water off. Place potatoes back in pot and add The Legendary Cheryl Scott's seasoning, salt, pepper, and minced garlic. Also add garlic butter and toss the red potatoes so all the good seasoning is all over. Last but not least I add some fresh parsley on top. And there you have it!

RUTH THE TOOT FAVORITE (IN LOVING MEMORIES OF MY MOM RUTH SCOTT MACKEY)

INGREDIENTS
Red bell peppers, Yellow bell peppers, Bay leaves, The Legendary Cheryl Scott's seasoning mild or spicy, Cayenne pepper, Shrimps, Georgia mild hot or mild sausages, Uncle Ben's white rice, Tomato sauce, Tomato paste, Thyme, Onions

HOW IT'S MADE
Fry some red bell peppers, green bell peppers, Georgia mild sausages in some olive oil then add some tomato sauce, tomato paste, 3 cups of water and some cayenne pepper, Add Uncle Ben's white rice to a pot of boiling water and let boil for approximately 20 to 25 minutes, then turn stove on medium low. Sauté some shrimps in some olive oil with my Legendary Cheryl Scott's seasoning, then stir the pot and add in the shrimps allow it to continue cooking for about another 10 minutes. When rice is finish cooking add in the stir fry with the rice and mix altogether. And there you have it. My mom's favorite.

SANDY'S SALMON WITH A TWIST

INGREDIENTS
Medium size salmon, Garlic butter, Parsley flakes, Real lemon, Heavy whip cream, Red peppers, The Legendary Cheryl Scott's seasoning spicy or mild, Lemon pepper

HOW IT'S MADE
Season salmon with the Legendary Cheryl Scott's spicy seasoning and let sit for a minute. Use a large skillet to heat some garlic butter then add in seasoned salmon fillet and let cook for approximately 2 to 3 minutes on each side. Then add in red peppers, fresh squeeze lemon, onions, garlic butter and let cook for an additional 3 to 4 minutes, add heavy whipping cream. Put onions on top and there you have it! You can either put it over a bed of fresh lettuce and spinach or a bed of white rice, or some mashed potatoes whichever one you prefer

SARAH'S BRUNCH

INGREDIENTS
Shrimps, Broccoli, Green onions, Fresh garlic, Legendary Cheryl Scott's spicy seasoning, Salmon, Garlic butter, Olive oil

HOW IT'S MADE
Season salmon steaks and shrimps with the Legendary Cheryl Scott's seasoning. Put seasoned salmon steaks first in aluminum pan and then place shrimps over salmon steak. Cut up some green onions, fresh garlic, fresh parsley, and broccoli and sauté them in olive oil and garlic butter to make a sauce. Take sauce and pour on top of the seasoned salmon steaks and shrimps. Set oven to 375° and let it bake until golden brown and there you have it

SONYA'S SPECIAL

INGREDIENTS
Eggs, Bacon, Ham, Chicken, Baby spinach, Salt and pepper, Legendary Cheryl Scott's mild or spicy seasoning, American yellow cheese, Olive oil

HOW IT'S MADE
Heat some olive oil in a large frying pan, once pan is heated put some eggs, then add either ham, chicken, or bacon (your choice), baby spinach, American cheese, sprinkle a little Legendary Cheryl Scott's mild seasoning, a little salt and pepper and let simmer for about 2 to 3 minutes. Remove from frying pan, fold it in half and place in a dish and there you have it.

SHENNETTE'S SHRIMP NOODLE PASTA

INGREDIENTS
Thin noodles, Shrimps, Red and Orange bell peppers, Olive oil, Diced onions, Diced celery, Soy sauce, The Legendary Cheryl Scott's Seasoning, Red pepper flakes

HOW IT'S MADE
First boil some pasta noodles. then set them aside. Next in a medium frying pan I add some olive oil and stir fry the orange, red bell peppers, dice onions, some dice celery and stir it altogether. Then I add the cooked pasta noodles. Last but not least add a little bit of soy sauce. Let simmer for around 2 to 3 minutes and Wala there you have it.

JACQUELINE'S SHRIMPER LICIOUS

INGREDIENTS
Large Jumbo shrimps, Red bell peppers, Garlic butter, The Legendary Cheryl Scott's seasoning, Olive oil, Butter

HOW IT'S MADE
In a medium skillet with some olive oil sauté some bell peppers and onions in some butter. Add some garlic butter along with large jumbo shrimps. Let cook 3 to 4 minutes and there you have it. I put it over a bit of hot white grits.

THAT'S MY VANILLA DIVA

INGREDIENTS
Georgia sausages mild, Medium Shrimps, Italian sausage, Red bell peppers, Green onions, Red pepper flakes, Butter, Olive oil, Legendary Cheryl Scott's seasoning mild or spicy

HOW IT'S MADE
Fry some Georgia sausage and Italian sausage, set them aside and boil some large noodles. While noodles are boiling in a saucepan add some olive oil, butter, green onions, red bell peppers, red pepper seeds and stir fry it to approximately 2 to 3 minutes. Add in cooked Georgia and Italian sausages. Then add in the cook noodles to the pan and more butter and more red pepper seeds and there you have it. Absolutely marvelous

WONNY THAT LOOKS DELICIOUS

INGREDIENTS
Shrimp, Chicken, Jerk seasoning, Legendary Cheryl Scott's seasoning mild or spicy, Olive oil

HOW IT'S MADE
Put some olive oil in the frying pan, while the frying pan is warming up add jerk seasoning to chicken chunks along with some shrimps. Add both the shrimp and chicken to the medium frying pan. Add some of The Legendary Cheryl Scott's seasoning. Also add a little bit more jerk seasoning and toss it for about 3 to 5 minutes and there you have it you can eat it with tacos or on a bed or rice.

YOU BETTER BELIEVE IT

INGREDIENTS
Stewed tomatoes, Shrimp, Fresh okra, Green bell peppers, Onions, Yellow bell peppers, Tomato sauce, Tomato paste, The Legendary Cheryl Scott's Seasoning spicy or mild

HOW IT'S MADE
Chop up some green and yellow bell peppers and onions. Stir-fry in a pan then add in stew tomatoes, three cans of tomato sauce and one can of tomato paste. Add in 2 cups of water then bring to a boil. Add in freshly cut up okra let simmer for about 20 minutes add fresh large shrimps. Cover pot and turn off the stove because the steam will cook the shrimps. You either eat it that way or you could eat it over a bed of rice, or a bowl of grits. There you have it..Enjoy!

THIS IS WHAT I'M TALKIN ABOUT

INGREDIENTS
Fresh okra, Onions, Stewed tomatoes, Green bell peppers, Cayenne pepper, The Legendary Cheryl Scott's seasoning, Bahamian conch, Vegetable oil

HOW IT'S MADE
Tenderize conch until soft. Fry conch and set aside next, stir fry some diced bell peppers, onions along with some stewed tomatoes add in 2 cups of water and bring to a boil for 5 minutes and let simmer. Add in conch to the pot. You can either eat this over a bed of pigeon peas and rice or a bed of white rice. There you have it!

ZACHARIAH PIGEON PEAS AND RICE

INGREDIENTS
Pigeon peas, Bell peppers, Salt and black pepper, Legendary Cheryl Scott's seasoning mild or spicy, Uncle Ben rice, Crisco oil

HOW IT'S MADE
Fry some bell peppers in a pan with some Crisco oil, then add 1 can of tomato paste, 3 cans of tomato sauce. When making a large pan like this use 5 cups of water. Bring rice to a boil with the pigeon peas added and salt, black pepper, and a dash of Legendary Cheryl Scott's seasoning. Let it cook until done or about 25 minutes. Watch the pot carefully if you wanted to come out looking like this. I name this dish after my Stepfather Zachariah because he made a fresh pot of pigeon peas and rice every single day.

Lightning Source UK Ltd.
Milton Keynes UK
UKHW051028211122
412556UK00009B/60